PASSWORD JOURNAL
AND WEBSITE KEEPER

Copyright 2015

All Rights reserved. No part of this book may be reproduced or used in any way or form or by any means whether electronic or mechanical, this means that you cannot record or photocopy any material ideas or tips that are provided in this book.

CALENDAR

JANUARY

FEBRUARY

MARCH

APRIL

MAY

JUNE

JULY

AUGUST

SEPTEMBER

OCTOBER

NOVEMBER

DECEMBER

Username
Password
Email

Username
Password
Email

Username
Password
Email

Username
Password
Email

Username
Password
Email

Username
Password
Email

Username
Password
Email

Username
Password
Email

Username
Password
Email

Username
Password
Email

Username
Password
Email

Username
Password
Email

Username	
Password	
Email	

Username	
Password	
Email	

Username	
Password	
Email	

Username	
Password	
Email	

Username	
Password	
Email	

Username	
Password	
Email	

Username	
Password	
Email	

Username	
Password	
Email	

Username	
Password	
Email	

Username	
Password	
Email	

Username	
Password	
Email	

Username	
Password	
Email	

Username	
Password	
Email	

Username	
Password	
Email	

Username
Password
Email

Username
Password
Email

Username
Password
Email

Username
Password
Email

Username
Password
Email

Username
Password
Email

Username
Password
Email

Username
Password
Email

Username
Password
Email

Username
Password
Email

Username
Password
Email

Username
Password
Email

Username
Password
Email

Username
Password
Email

Username	
Password	
Email	

Username	
Password	
Email	

Username	
Password	
Email	

Username	
Password	
Email	

Username	
Password	
Email	

Username	
Password	
Email	

Username	
Password	
Email	

Username	
Password	
Email	

Username	
Password	
Email	

Username	
Password	
Email	

Username	
Password	
Email	

Username	
Password	
Email	

Username
Password
Email

Username
Password
Email

Username
Password
Email

Username
Password
Email

Username
Password
Email

Username
Password
Email

Username
Password
Email

Username
Password
Email

Username
Password
Email

Username
Password
Email

Username
Password
Email

Username
Password
Email

Username
Password
Email

Username
Password
Email

Username
Password
Email

Username
Password
Email

Username
Password
Email

Username
Password
Email

Username
Password
Email

Username
Password
Email

Username
Password
Email

Username
Password
Email

Username
Password
Email

Username
Password
Email

Username
Password
Email

Username
Password
Email

Username
Password
Email

Username
Password
Email

Username		Username
Password		Password
Email		Email

Username		Username
Password		Password
Email		Email

Username		Username
Password		Password
Email		Email

Username		Username
Password		Password
Email		Email

Username		Username
Password		Password
Email		Email

Username		Username
Password		Password
Email		Email

Username		Username
Password		Password
Email		Email

Username	
Password	
Email	

Username	
Password	
Email	

Username	
Password	
Email	

Username	
Password	
Email	

Username	
Password	
Email	

Username	
Password	
Email	

Username	
Password	
Email	

Username	
Password	
Email	

Username	
Password	
Email	

Username	
Password	
Email	

Username	
Password	
Email	

Username	
Password	
Email	

Username	
Password	
Email	

Username	
Password	
Email	

Username
Password
Email

Username
Password
Email

Username
Password
Email

Username
Password
Email

Username
Password
Email

Username
Password
Email

Username
Password
Email

Username
Password
Email

Username
Password
Email

Username
Password
Email

Username
Password
Email

Username
Password
Email

Username	
Password	
Email	

Username	
Password	
Email	

Username	
Password	
Email	

Username	
Password	
Email	

Username	
Password	
Email	

Username	
Password	
Email	

Username	
Password	
Email	

Username	
Password	
Email	

Username	
Password	
Email	

Username	
Password	
Email	

Username	
Password	
Email	

Username	
Password	
Email	

Username	
Password	
Email	

Username	
Password	
Email	

Username	Username
Password	Password
Email	Email

Username	Username
Password	Password
Email	Email

Username	Username
Password	Password
Email	Email

Username	Username
Password	Password
Email	Email

Username	Username
Password	Password
Email	Email

Username	Username
Password	Password
Email	Email

Username	Username
Password	Password
Email	Email

Username		Username
Password		Password
Email		Email

Username		Username
Password		Password
Email		Email

Username		Username
Password		Password
Email		Email

Username		Username
Password		Password
Email		Email

Username		Username
Password		Password
Email		Email

Username		Username
Password		Password
Email		Email

Username		Username
Password		Password
Email		Email

Username	Username
Password	Password
Email	Email

Username	Username
Password	Password
Email	Email

Username	Username
Password	Password
Email	Email

Username	Username
Password	Password
Email	Email

Username	Username
Password	Password
Email	Email

Username	Username
Password	Password
Email	Email

Username	Username
Password	Password
Email	Email

Username
Password
Email

Username
Password
Email

Username
Password
Email

Username
Password
Email

Username
Password
Email

Username
Password
Email

Username
Password
Email

Username
Password
Email

Username
Password
Email

Username
Password
Email

Username
Password
Email

Username
Password
Email

Username
Password
Email

Username
Password
Email

Username
Password
Email

Username
Password
Email

Username
Password
Email

Username
Password
Email

Username
Password
Email

Username
Password
Email

Username
Password
Email

Username
Password
Email

Username
Password
Email

Username
Password
Email

Username
Password
Email

Username
Password
Email

Username
Password
Email

Username
Password
Email

Username	
Password	
Email	

Username	
Password	
Email	

Username	
Password	
Email	

Username	
Password	
Email	

Username	
Password	
Email	

Username	
Password	
Email	

Username	
Password	
Email	

Username	
Password	
Email	

Username	
Password	
Email	

Username	
Password	
Email	

Username	
Password	
Email	

Username	
Password	
Email	

Username	
Password	
Email	

Username	
Password	
Email	

Username
Password
Email

Username
Password
Email

Username
Password
Email

Username
Password
Email

Username
Password
Email

Username
Password
Email

Username
Password
Email

Username
Password
Email

Username
Password
Email

Username
Password
Email

Username
Password
Email

Username
Password
Email

Username	Username
Password	Password
Email	Email

Username	Username
Password	Password
Email	Email

Username	Username
Password	Password
Email	Email

Username	Username
Password	Password
Email	Email

Username	Username
Password	Password
Email	Email

Username	Username
Password	Password
Email	Email

Username	Username
Password	Password
Email	Email

Username	Username
Password	Password
Email	Email

Username	Username
Password	Password
Email	Email

Username	Username
Password	Password
Email	Email

Username	Username
Password	Password
Email	Email

Username	Username
Password	Password
Email	Email

Username	Username
Password	Password
Email	Email

Username	Username
Password	Password
Email	Email

Username
Password
Email

Username
Password
Email

Username
Password
Email

Username
Password
Email

Username
Password
Email

Username
Password
Email

Username
Password
Email

Username
Password
Email

Username
Password
Email

Username
Password
Email

Username
Password
Email

Username
Password
Email

Username
Password
Email

Username
Password
Email

Username
Password
Email

Username
Password
Email

Username
Password
Email

Username
Password
Email

Username
Password
Email

Username
Password
Email

Username
Password
Email

Username
Password
Email

Username
Password
Email

Username
Password
Email

Username
Password
Email

Username
Password
Email

Username	
Password	
Email	

Username	
Password	
Email	

Username	
Password	
Email	

Username	
Password	
Email	

Username	
Password	
Email	

Username	
Password	
Email	

Username	
Password	
Email	

Username	
Password	
Email	

Username	
Password	
Email	

Username	
Password	
Email	

Username	
Password	
Email	

Username	
Password	
Email	

Username	
Password	
Email	

Username	
Password	
Email	

Username
Password
Email

Username
Password
Email

Username
Password
Email

Username
Password
Email

Username
Password
Email

Username
Password
Email

Username
Password
Email

Username
Password
Email

Username
Password
Email

Username
Password
Email

Username
Password
Email

Username
Password
Email

Username
Password
Email

Username
Password
Email

Username
Password
Email

Username
Password
Email

Username
Password
Email

Username
Password
Email

Username
Password
Email

Username
Password
Email

Username
Password
Email

Username
Password
Email

Username
Password
Email

Username
Password
Email

Username
Password
Email

Username
Password
Email

Username
Password
Email

Username
Password
Email

Username
Password
Email

Username
Password
Email

Username
Password
Email

Username
Password
Email

Username
Password
Email

Username
Password
Email

Username
Password
Email

Username
Password
Email

Username
Password
Email

Username
Password
Email

Username
Password
Email

Username
Password
Email

Username
Password
Email

Username
Password
Email

Username
Password
Email

Username
Password
Email

Username
Password
Email

Username
Password
Email

Username
Password
Email

Username
Password
Email

Username
Password
Email

Username
Password
Email

Username
Password
Email

Username
Password
Email

Username
Password
Email

Username
Password
Email

Username
Password
Email

Username
Password
Email

Username
Password
Email

Username
Password
Email

Username
Password
Email

Username
Password
Email

Username
Password
Email

Username
Password
Email

Username
Password
Email

Username
Password
Email

Username	
Password	
Email	

Username	
Password	
Email	

Username	
Password	
Email	

Username	
Password	
Email	

Username	
Password	
Email	

Username	
Password	
Email	

Username	
Password	
Email	

Username	
Password	
Email	

Username	
Password	
Email	

Username	
Password	
Email	

Username	
Password	
Email	

Username	
Password	
Email	

Username	
Password	
Email	

Username	
Password	
Email	

Username	
Password	
Email	

Username	
Password	
Email	

Username	
Password	
Email	

Username	
Password	
Email	

Username	
Password	
Email	

Username	
Password	
Email	

Username	
Password	
Email	

Username	
Password	
Email	

Username	
Password	
Email	

Username	
Password	
Email	

Username	
Password	
Email	

Username	
Password	
Email	

Username
Password
Email

Username
Password
Email

Username
Password
Email

Username
Password
Email

Username
Password
Email

Username
Password
Email

Username
Password
Email

Username
Password
Email

Username
Password
Email

Username
Password
Email

Username
Password
Email

Username
Password
Email

Username
Password
Email

Username
Password
Email

Username
Password
Email

Username
Password
Email

Username
Password
Email

Username
Password
Email

Username
Password
Email

Username
Password
Email

Username
Password
Email

Username
Password
Email

Username
Password
Email

Username
Password
Email

Username
Password
Email

Username
Password
Email

Username
Password
Email

Username
Password
Email

Username
Password
Email

Username
Password
Email

Username
Password
Email

Username
Password
Email

Username
Password
Email

Username
Password
Email

Username
Password
Email

Username
Password
Email

Username
Password
Email

Username
Password
Email

Username
Password
Email

Username
Password
Email

Username
Password
Email

Username
Password
Email

Username		Username
Password		Password
Email		Email

Username		Username
Password		Password
Email		Email

Username		Username
Password		Password
Email		Email

Username		Username
Password		Password
Email		Email

Username		Username
Password		Password
Email		Email

Username		Username
Password		Password
Email		Email

Username		Username
Password		Password
Email		Email

Username	Username
Password	Password
Email	Email

Username	Username
Password	Password
Email	Email

Username	Username
Password	Password
Email	Email

Username	Username
Password	Password
Email	Email

Username	Username
Password	Password
Email	Email

Username	Username
Password	Password
Email	Email

Username	Username
Password	Password
Email	Email

Username
Password
Email

Username
Password
Email

Username
Password
Email

Username
Password
Email

Username
Password
Email

Username
Password
Email

Username
Password
Email

Username
Password
Email

Username
Password
Email

Username
Password
Email

Username
Password
Email

Username
Password
Email

Username
Password
Email

Username
Password
Email

Username	
Password	
Email	

Username	
Password	
Email	

Username	
Password	
Email	

Username	
Password	
Email	

Username	
Password	
Email	

Username	
Password	
Email	

Username	
Password	
Email	

Username	
Password	
Email	

Username	
Password	
Email	

Username	
Password	
Email	

Username	
Password	
Email	

Username	
Password	
Email	

Username	
Password	
Email	

Username	
Password	
Email	

Username	Username
Password	Password
Email	Email

Username	Username
Password	Password
Email	Email

Username	Username
Password	Password
Email	Email

Username	Username
Password	Password
Email	Email

Username	Username
Password	Password
Email	Email

Username	Username
Password	Password
Email	Email

Username	Username
Password	Password
Email	Email

Username	Username
Password	Password
Email	Email

Username	Username
Password	Password
Email	Email

Username	Username
Password	Password
Email	Email

Username	Username
Password	Password
Email	Email

Username	Username
Password	Password
Email	Email

Username	Username
Password	Password
Email	Email

Username	Username
Password	Password
Email	Email

Username
Password
Email

Username
Password
Email

Username
Password
Email

Username
Password
Email

Username
Password
Email

Username
Password
Email

Username
Password
Email

Username
Password
Email

Username
Password
Email

Username
Password
Email

Username
Password
Email

Username
Password
Email

Username	Username
Password	Password
Email	Email

Username	Username
Password	Password
Email	Email

Username	Username
Password	Password
Email	Email

Username	Username
Password	Password
Email	Email

Username	Username
Password	Password
Email	Email

Username	Username
Password	Password
Email	Email

Username	Username
Password	Password
Email	Email

Username
Password
Email

Username
Password
Email

Username
Password
Email

Username
Password
Email

Username
Password
Email

Username
Password
Email

Username
Password
Email

Username
Password
Email

Username
Password
Email

Username
Password
Email

Username
Password
Email

Username
Password
Email

Username	
Password	
Email	

Username	
Password	
Email	

Username	
Password	
Email	

Username	
Password	
Email	

Username	
Password	
Email	

Username	
Password	
Email	

Username	
Password	
Email	

Username	
Password	
Email	

Username	
Password	
Email	

Username	
Password	
Email	

Username	
Password	
Email	

Username	
Password	
Email	

Username	
Password	
Email	

Username	
Password	
Email	

Username	Username
Password	Password
Email	Email

Username	Username
Password	Password
Email	Email

Username	Username
Password	Password
Email	Email

Username	Username
Password	Password
Email	Email

Username	Username
Password	Password
Email	Email

Username	Username
Password	Password
Email	Email

Username	Username
Password	Password
Email	Email

Username		Username	
Password		Password	
Email		Email	

Username		Username	
Password		Password	
Email		Email	

Username		Username	
Password		Password	
Email		Email	

Username		Username	
Password		Password	
Email		Email	

Username		Username	
Password		Password	
Email		Email	

Username		Username	
Password		Password	
Email		Email	

Username		Username	
Password		Password	
Email		Email	

Username	Username
Password	Password
Email	Email

Username	Username
Password	Password
Email	Email

Username	Username
Password	Password
Email	Email

Username	Username
Password	Password
Email	Email

Username	Username
Password	Password
Email	Email

Username	Username
Password	Password
Email	Email

Username	Username
Password	Password
Email	Email

Username
Password
Email

Username
Password
Email

Username
Password
Email

Username
Password
Email

Username
Password
Email

Username
Password
Email

Username
Password
Email

Username
Password
Email

Username
Password
Email

Username
Password
Email

Username
Password
Email

Username
Password
Email

Username
Password
Email

Username
Password
Email

Username
Password
Email

Username
Password
Email

Username
Password
Email

Username
Password
Email

Username
Password
Email

Username
Password
Email

Username
Password
Email

Username
Password
Email

Username
Password
Email

Username
Password
Email

Username
Password
Email

Username
Password
Email

www.ingramcontent.com/pod-product-compliance
Lightning Source LLC
Chambersburg PA
CBHW060444060326
40690CB00019B/4333